MUSHROOM

COLORING BOOK FOR ADULTS

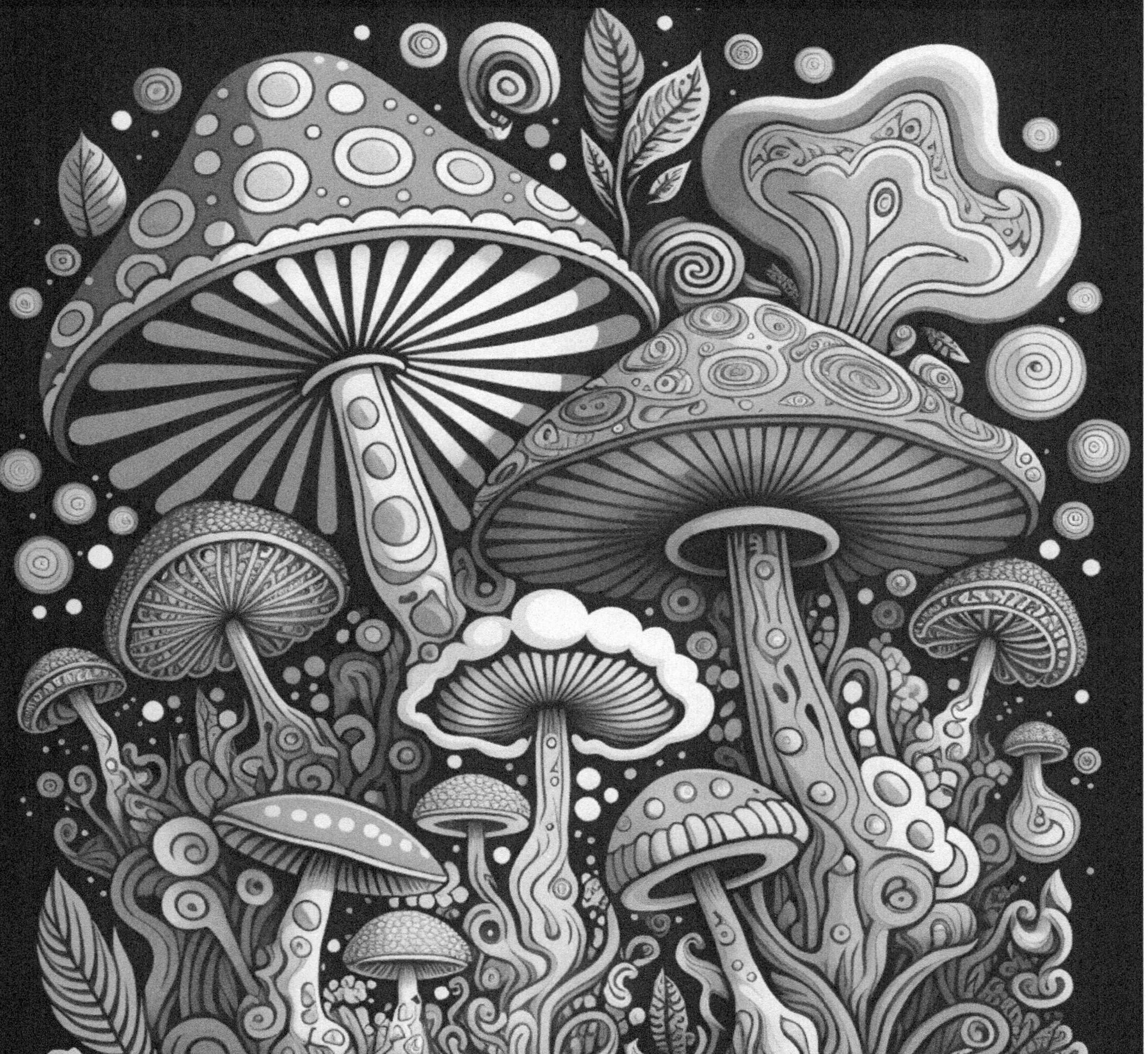

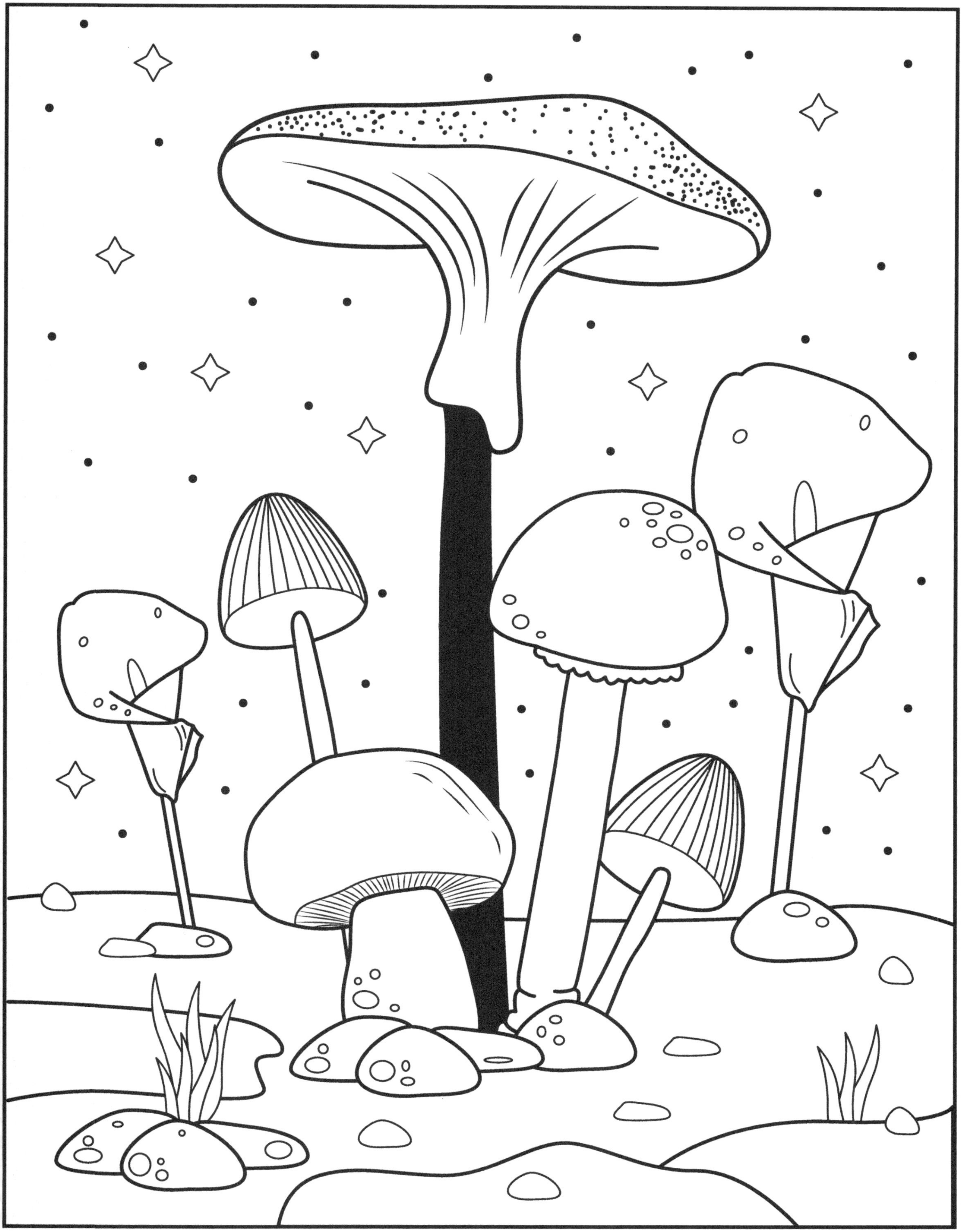

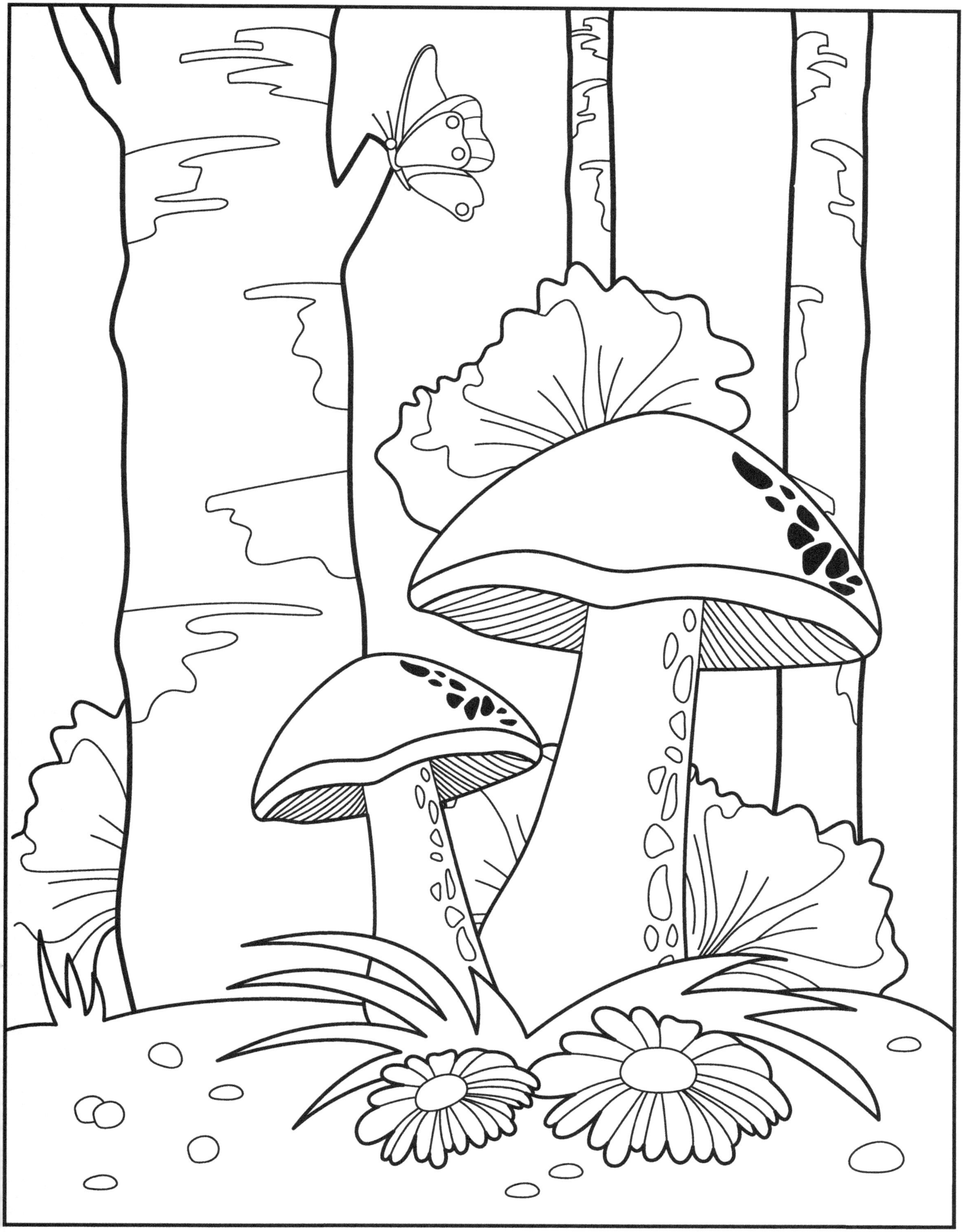

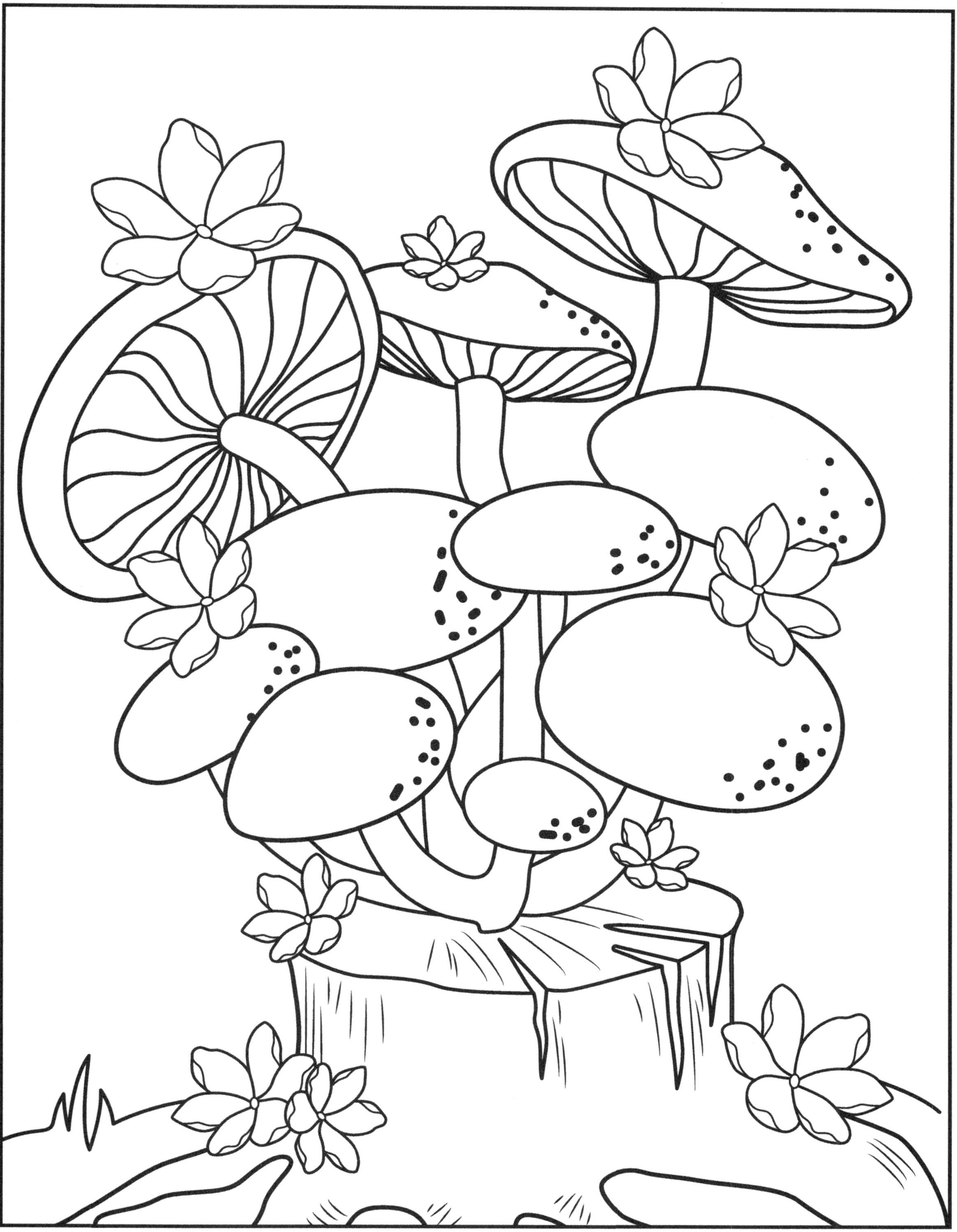

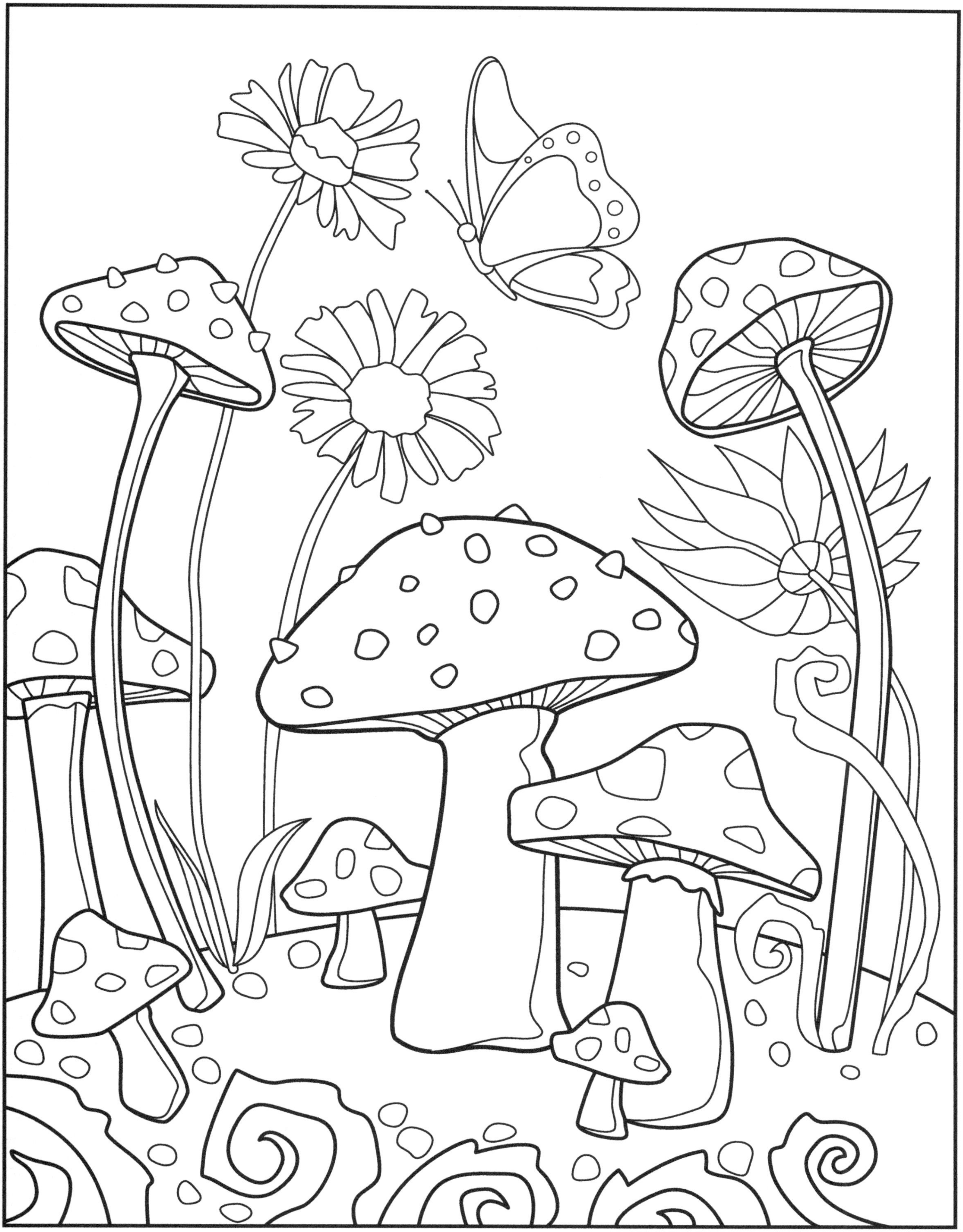

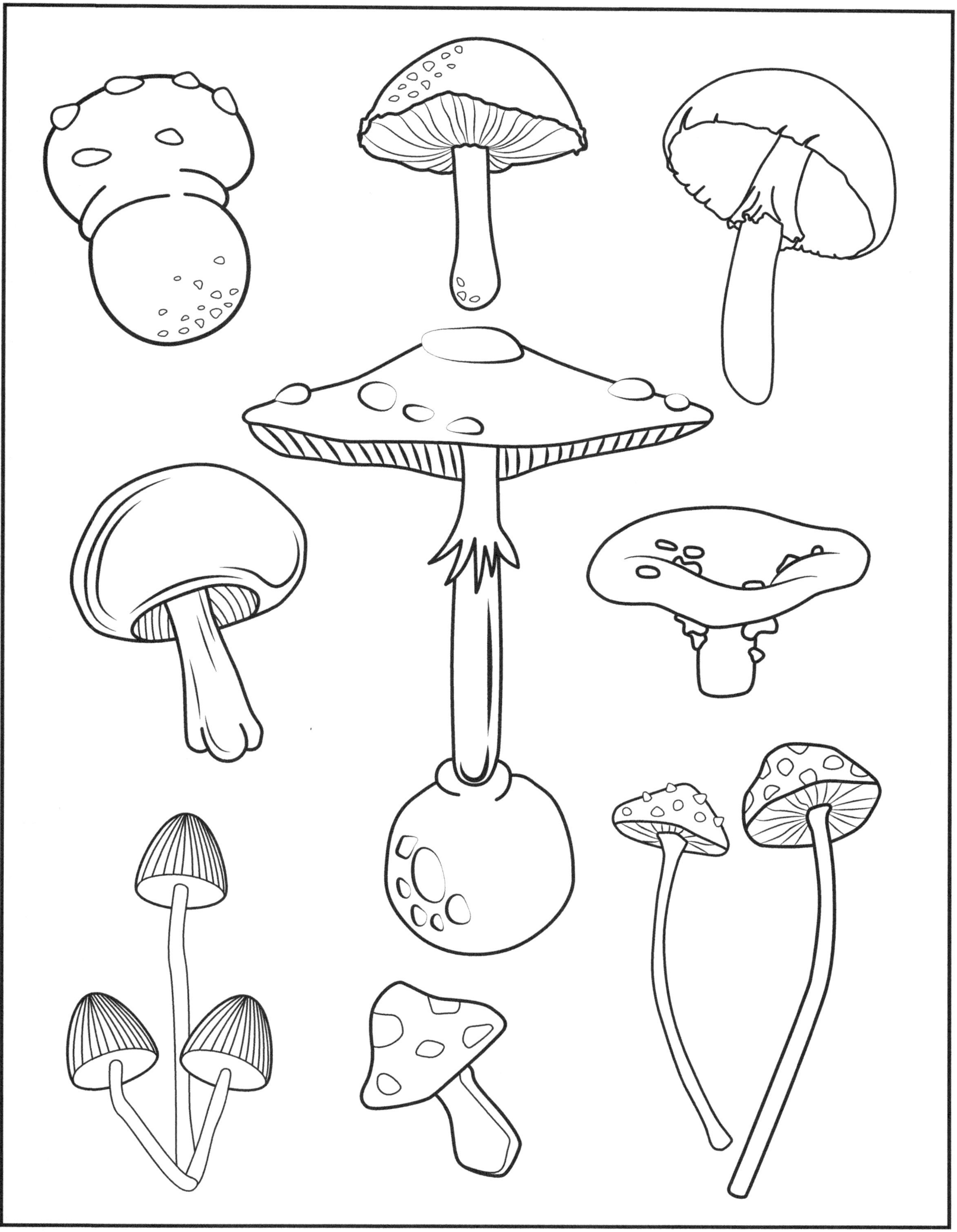

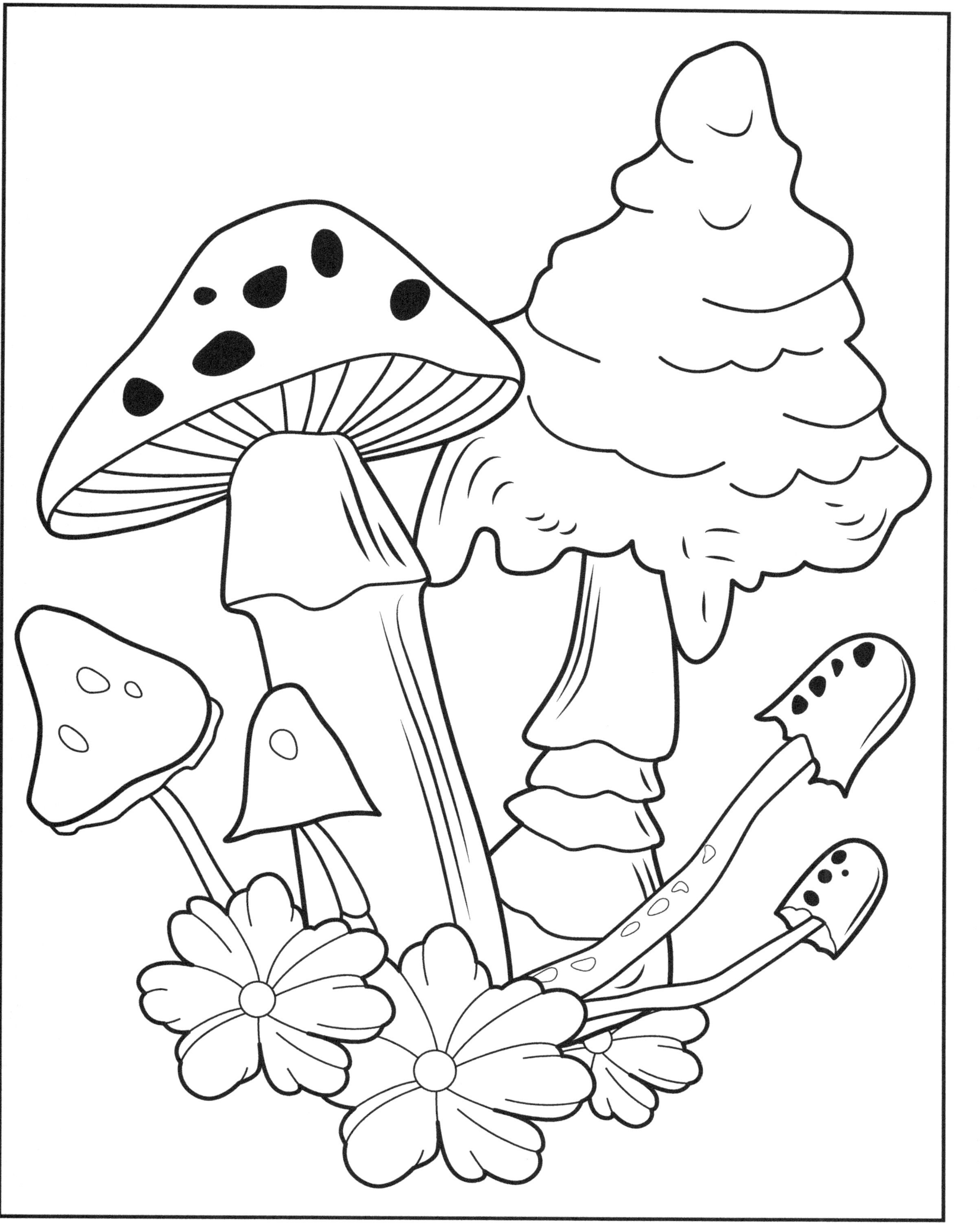

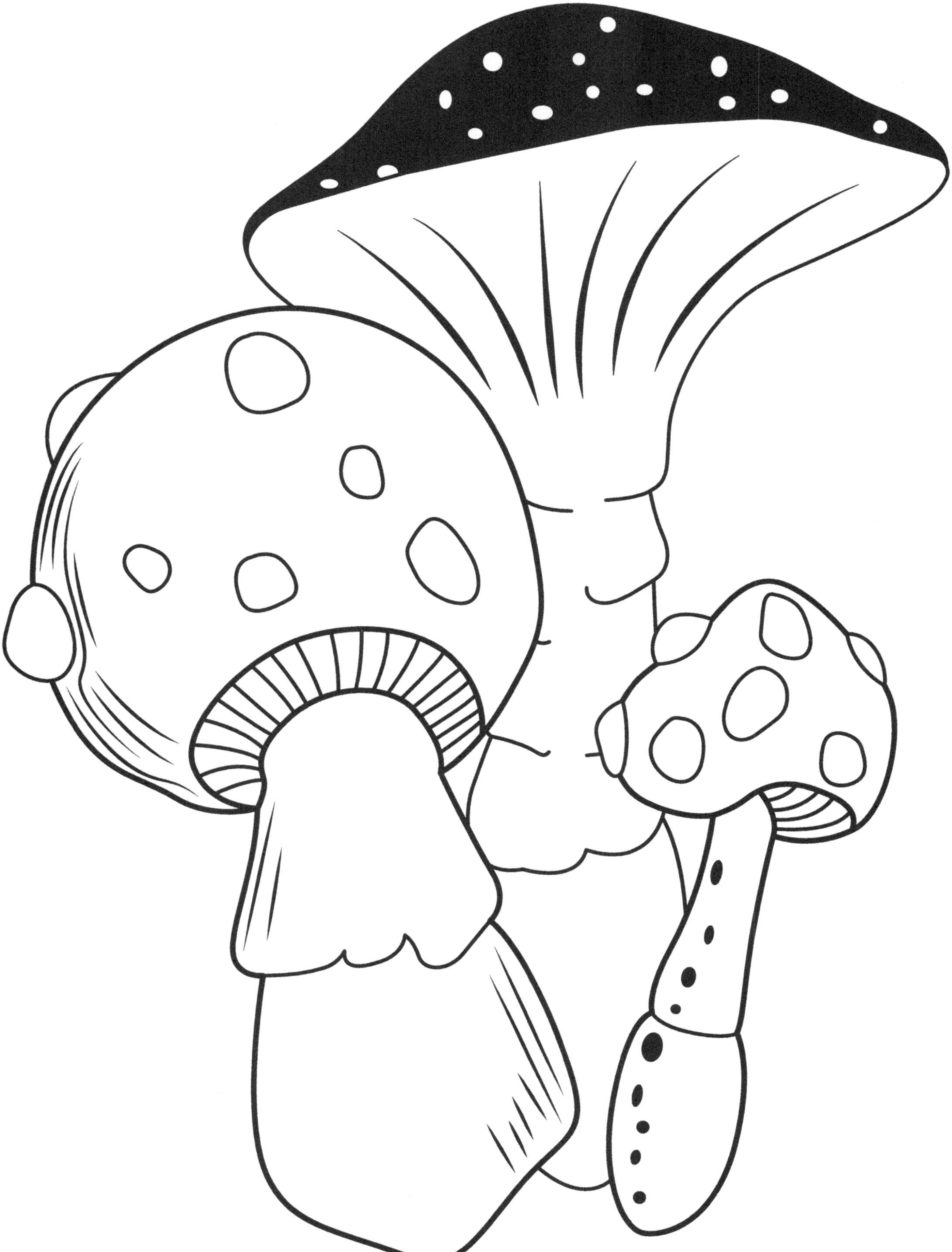

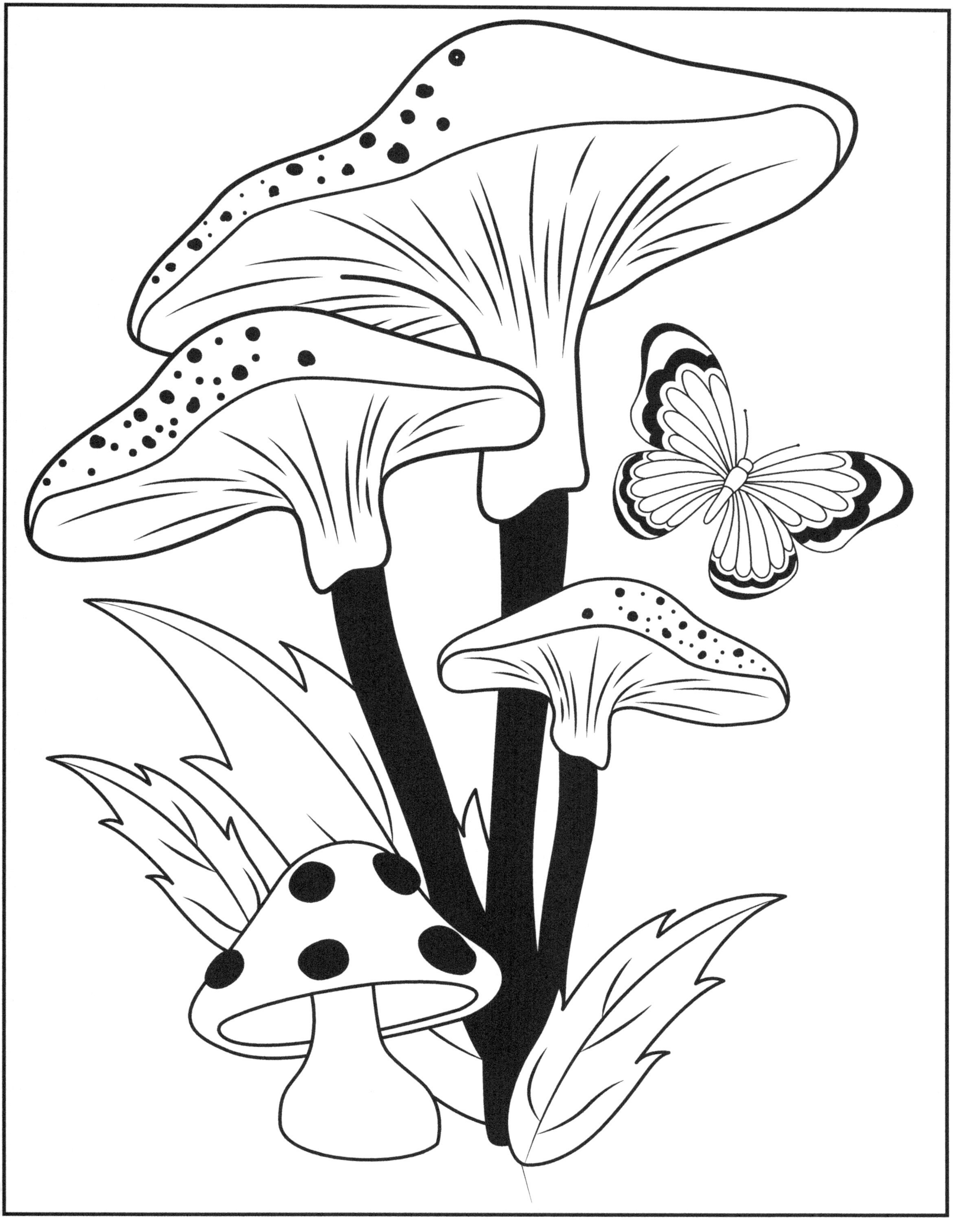

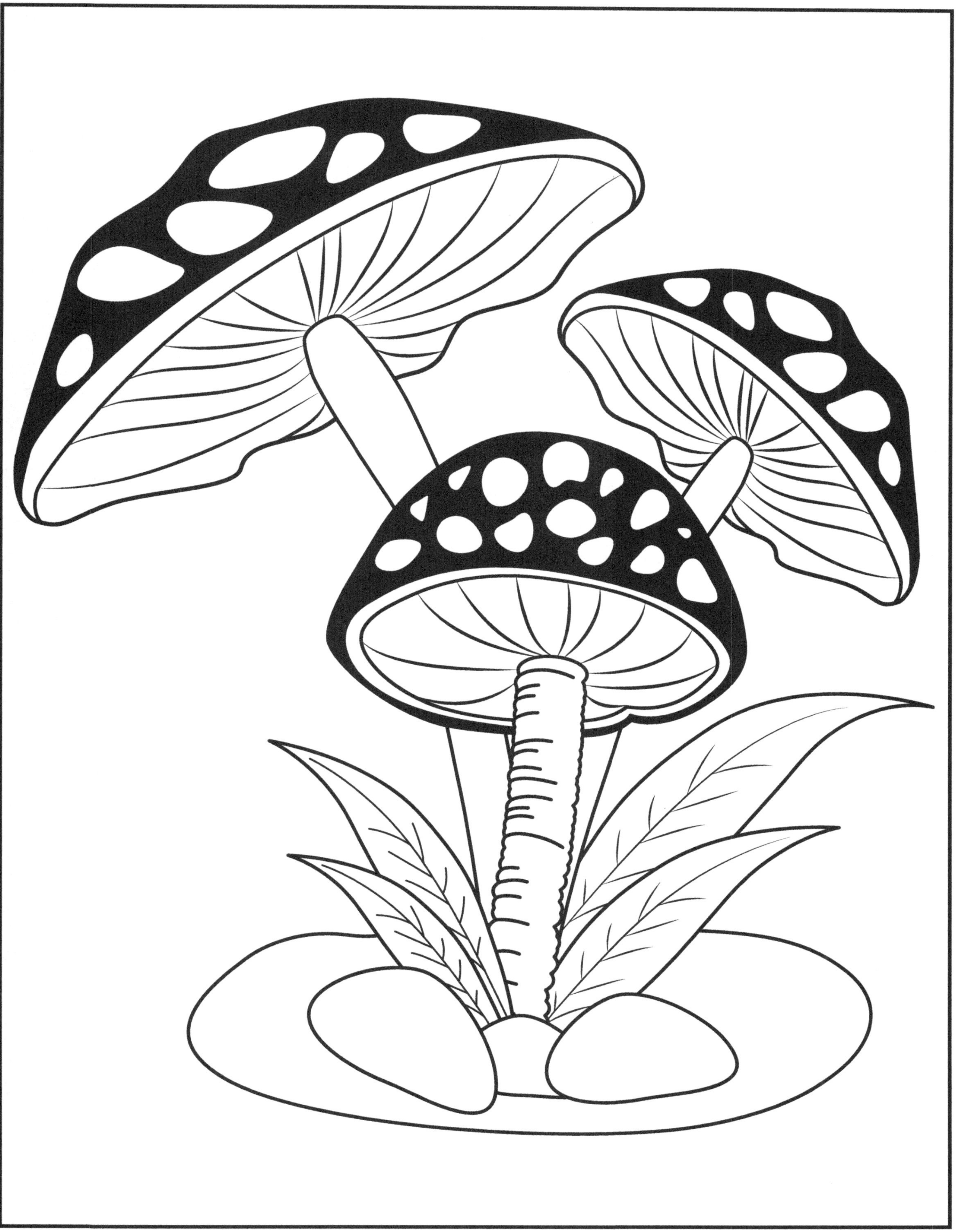

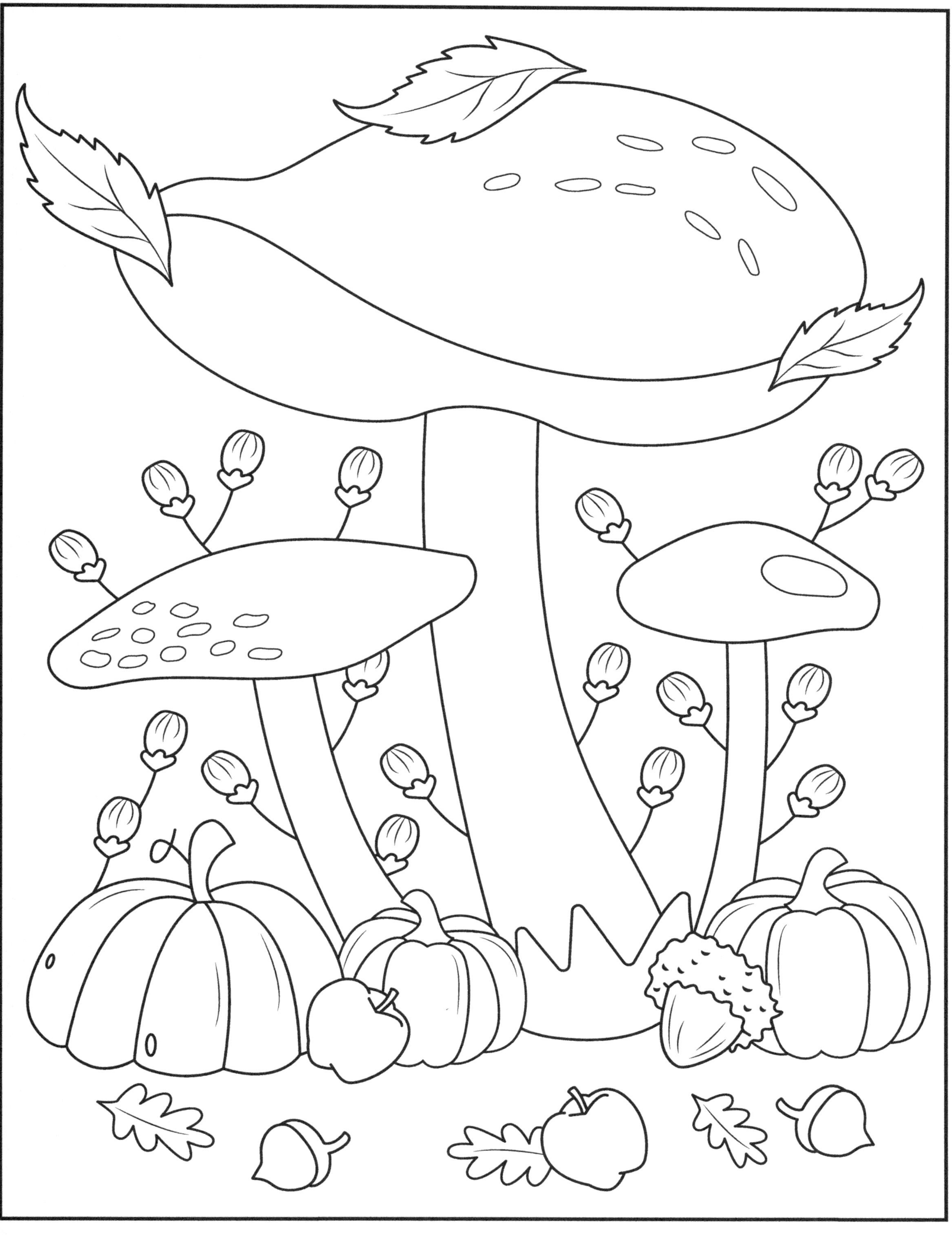

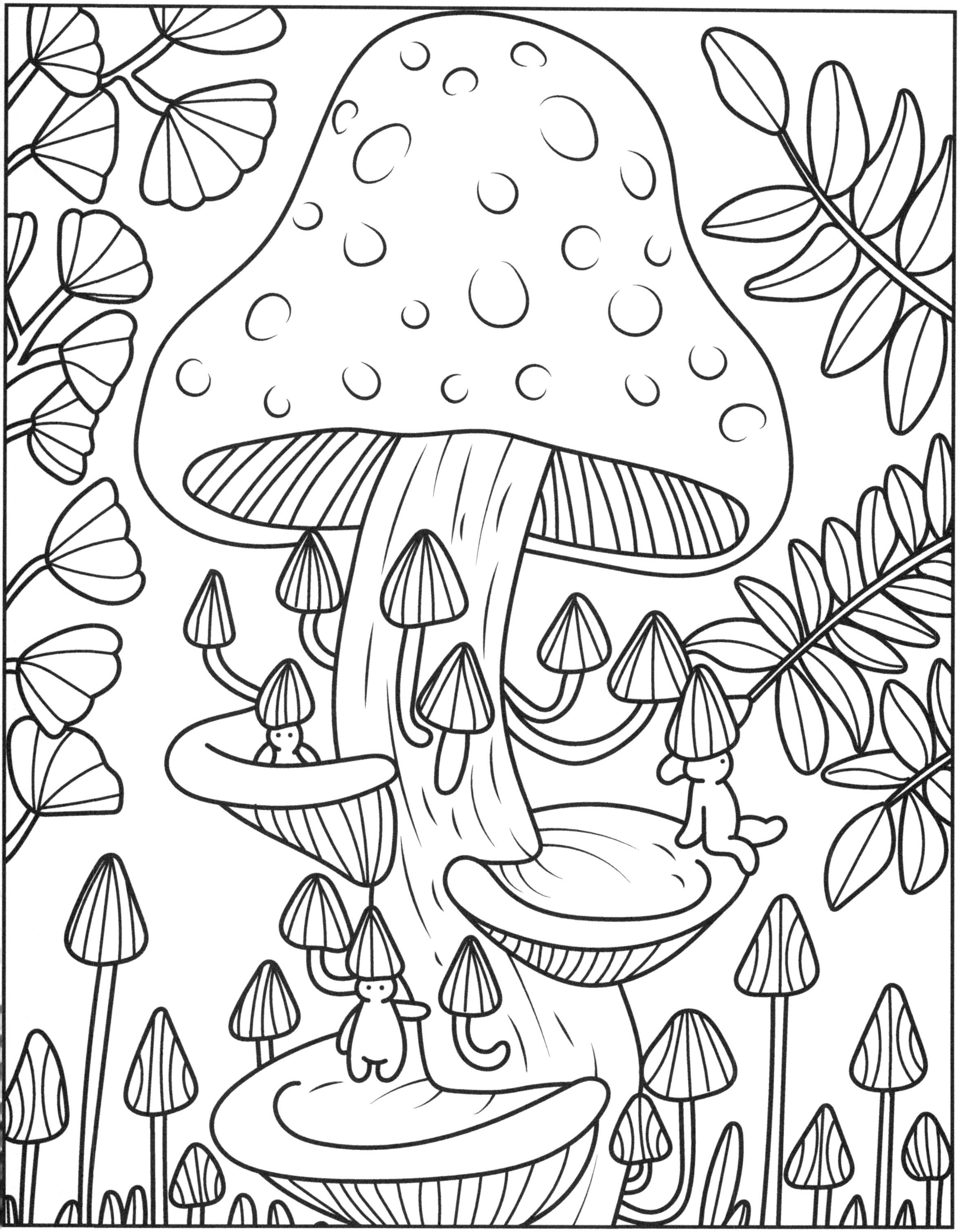

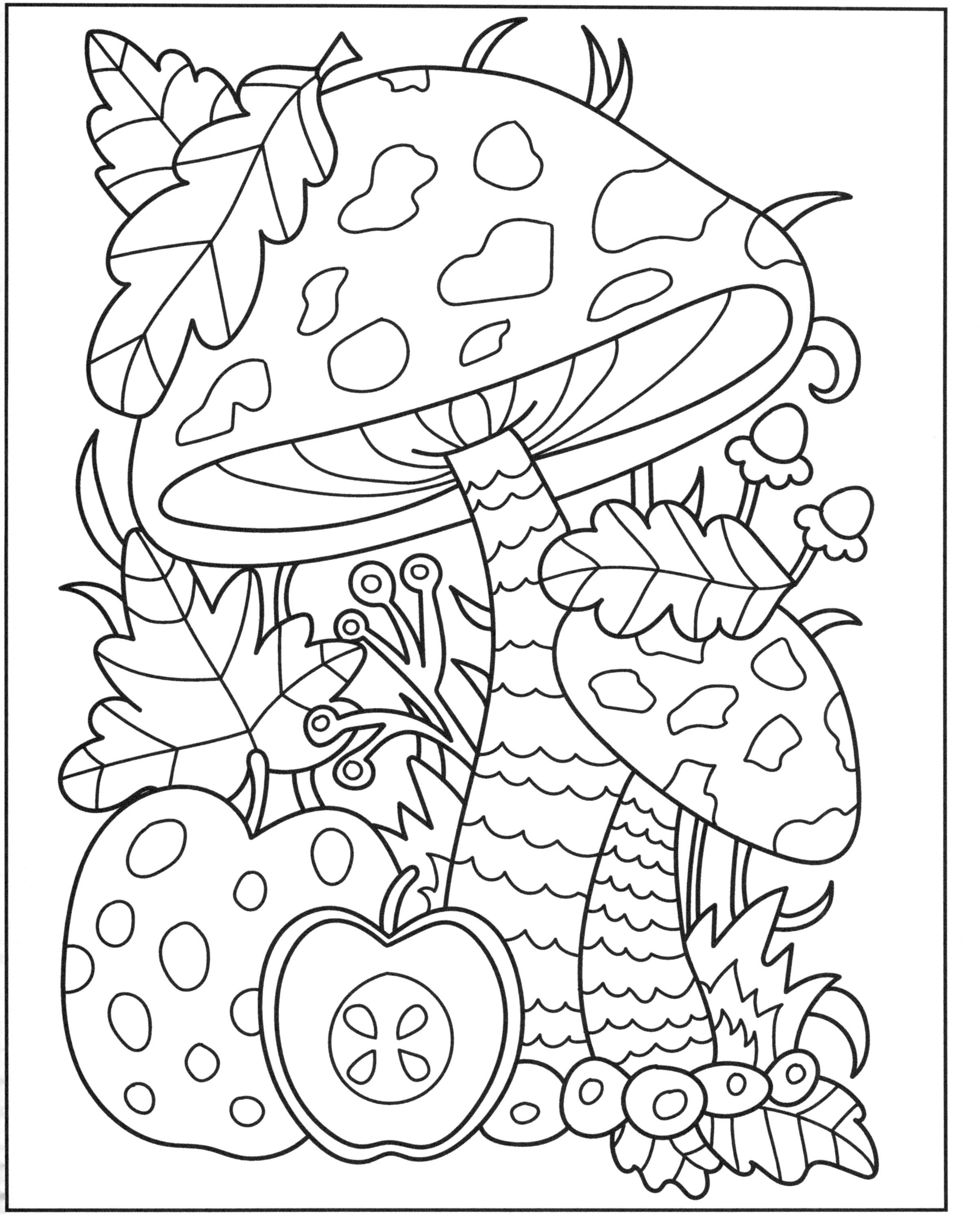

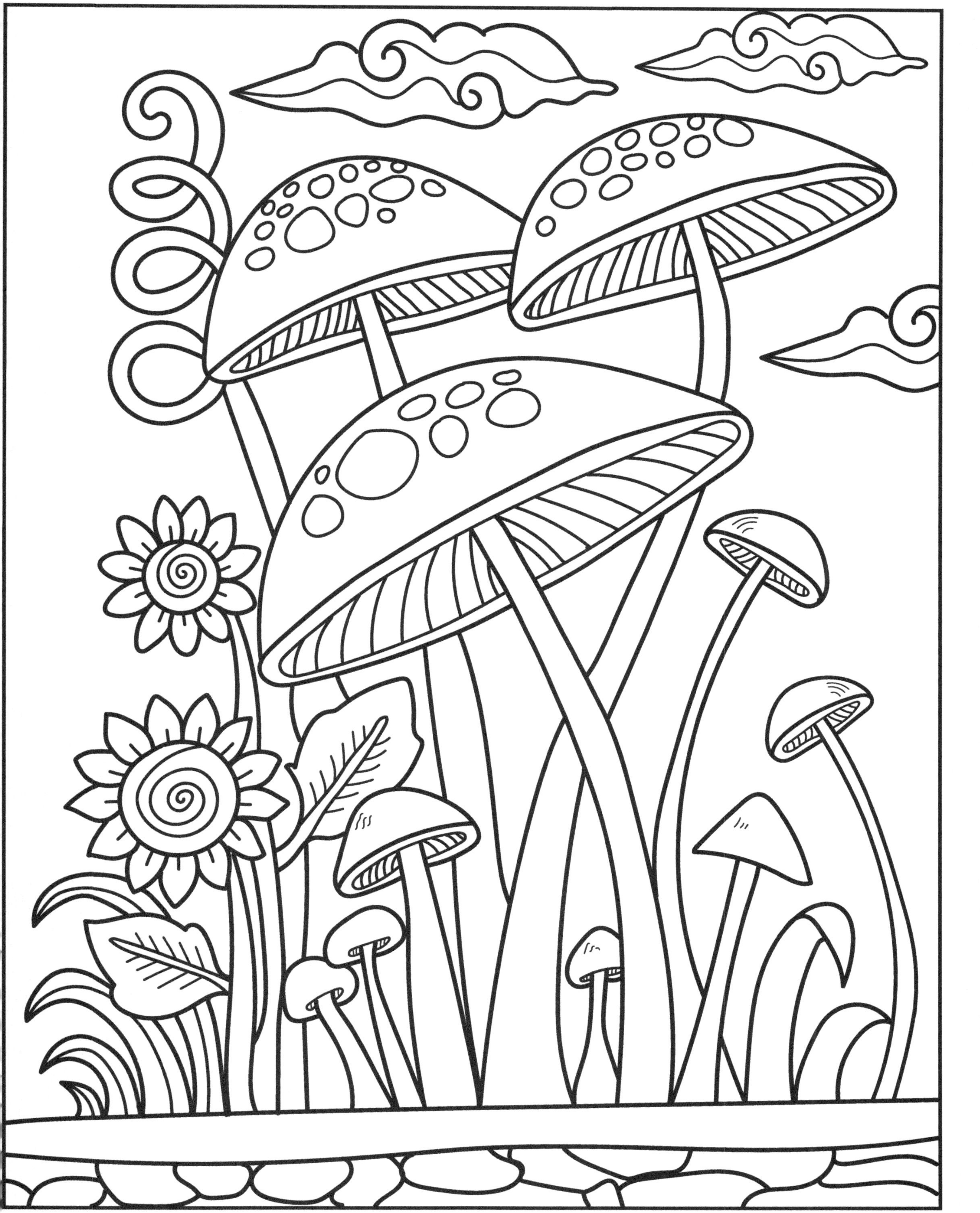

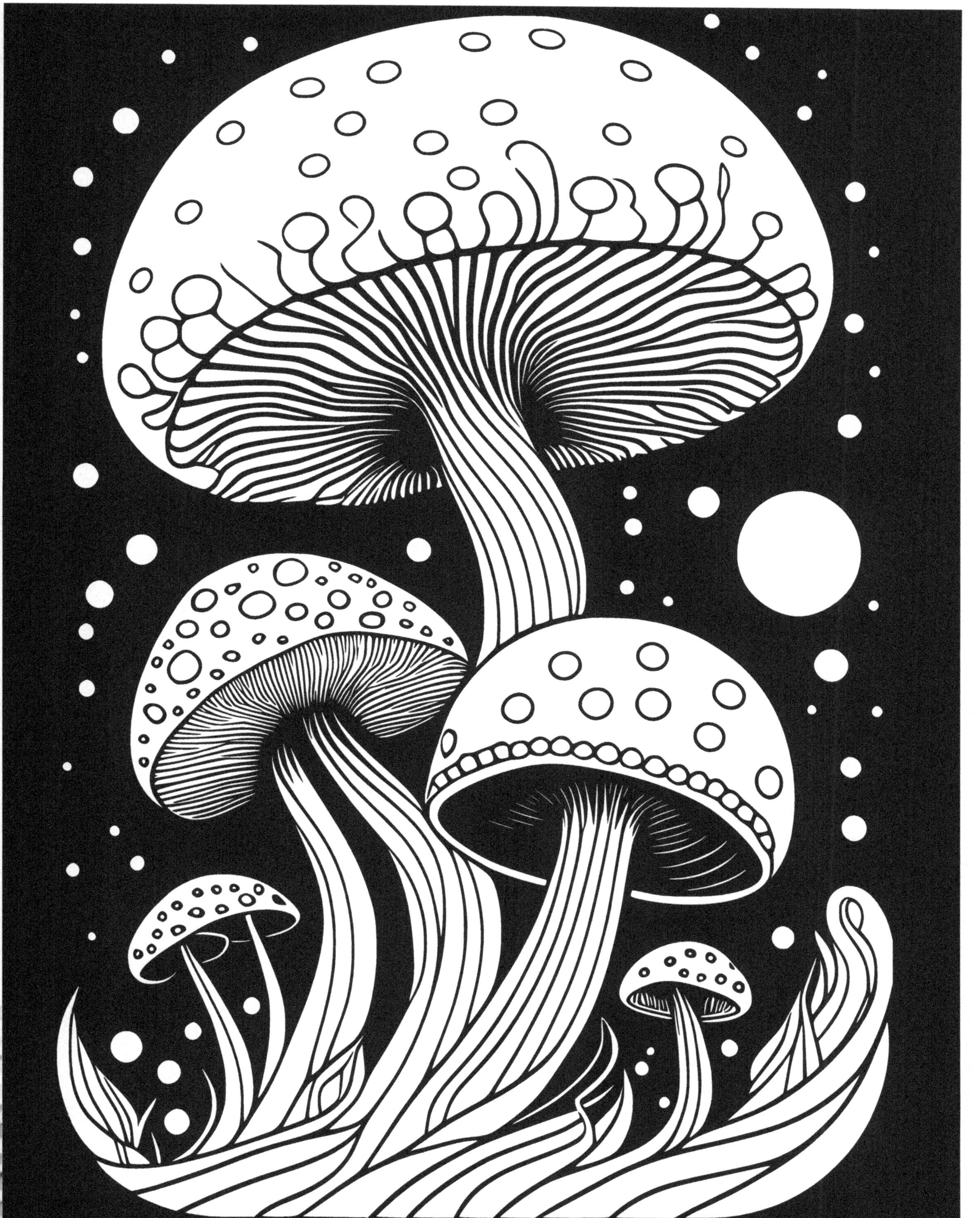

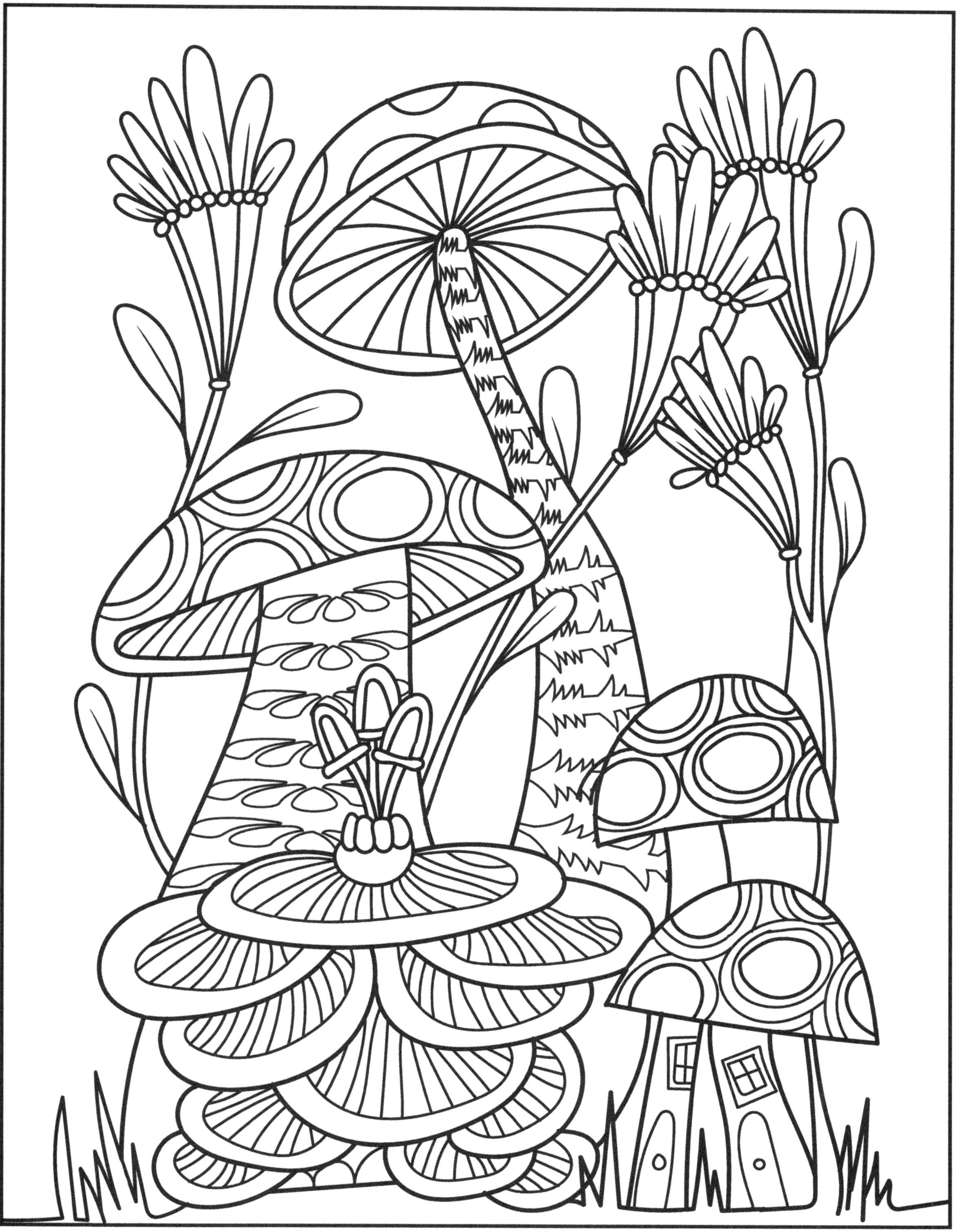

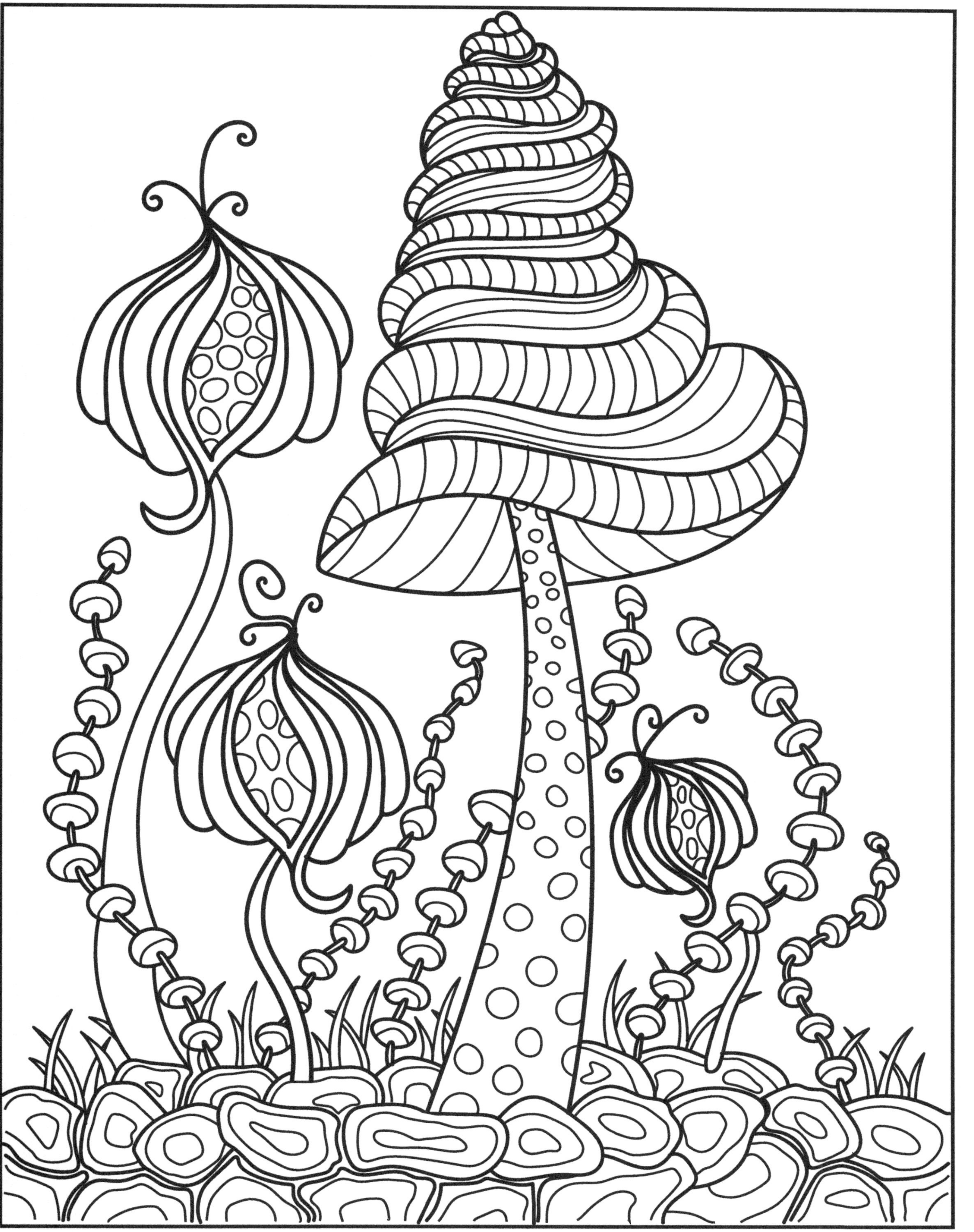

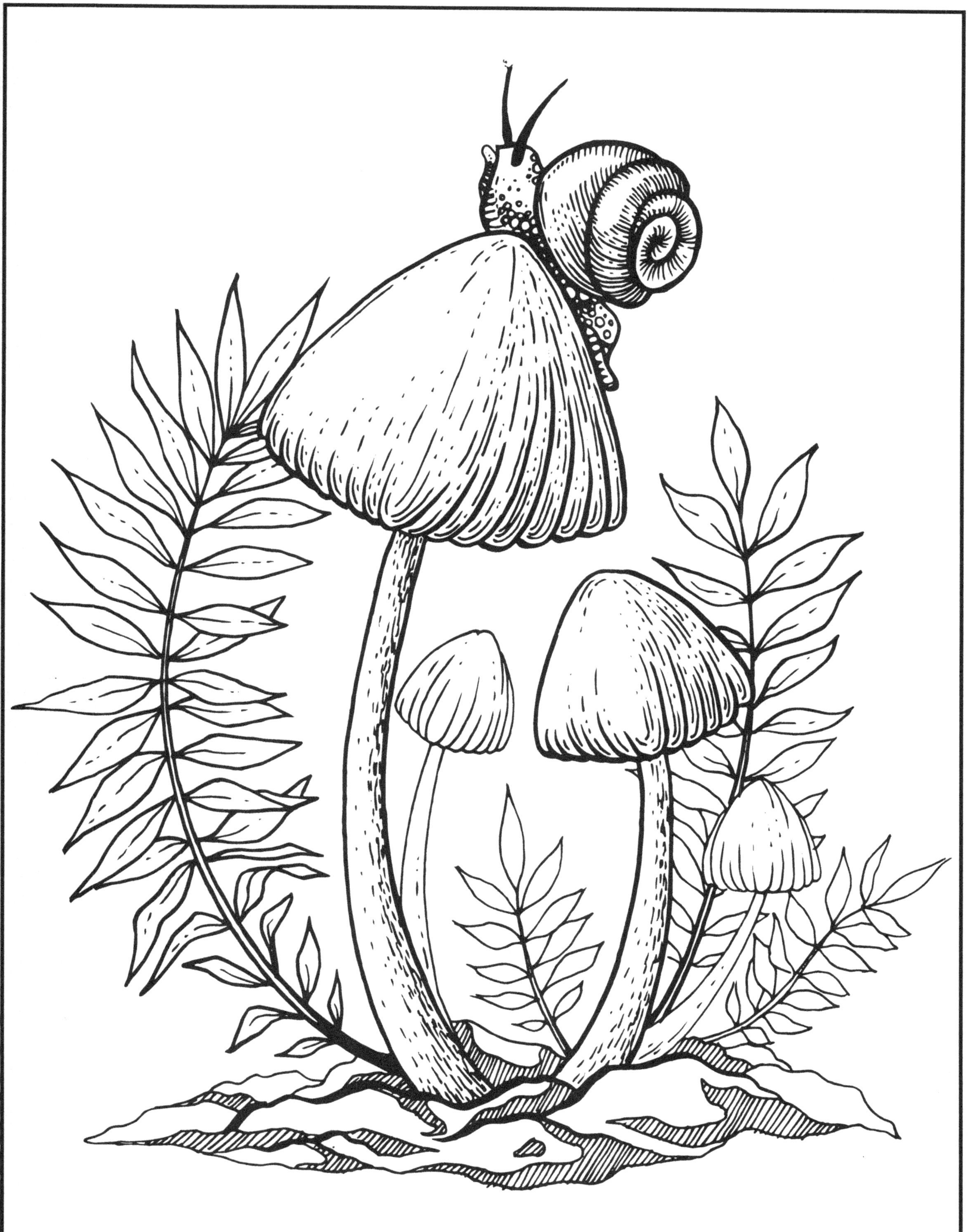

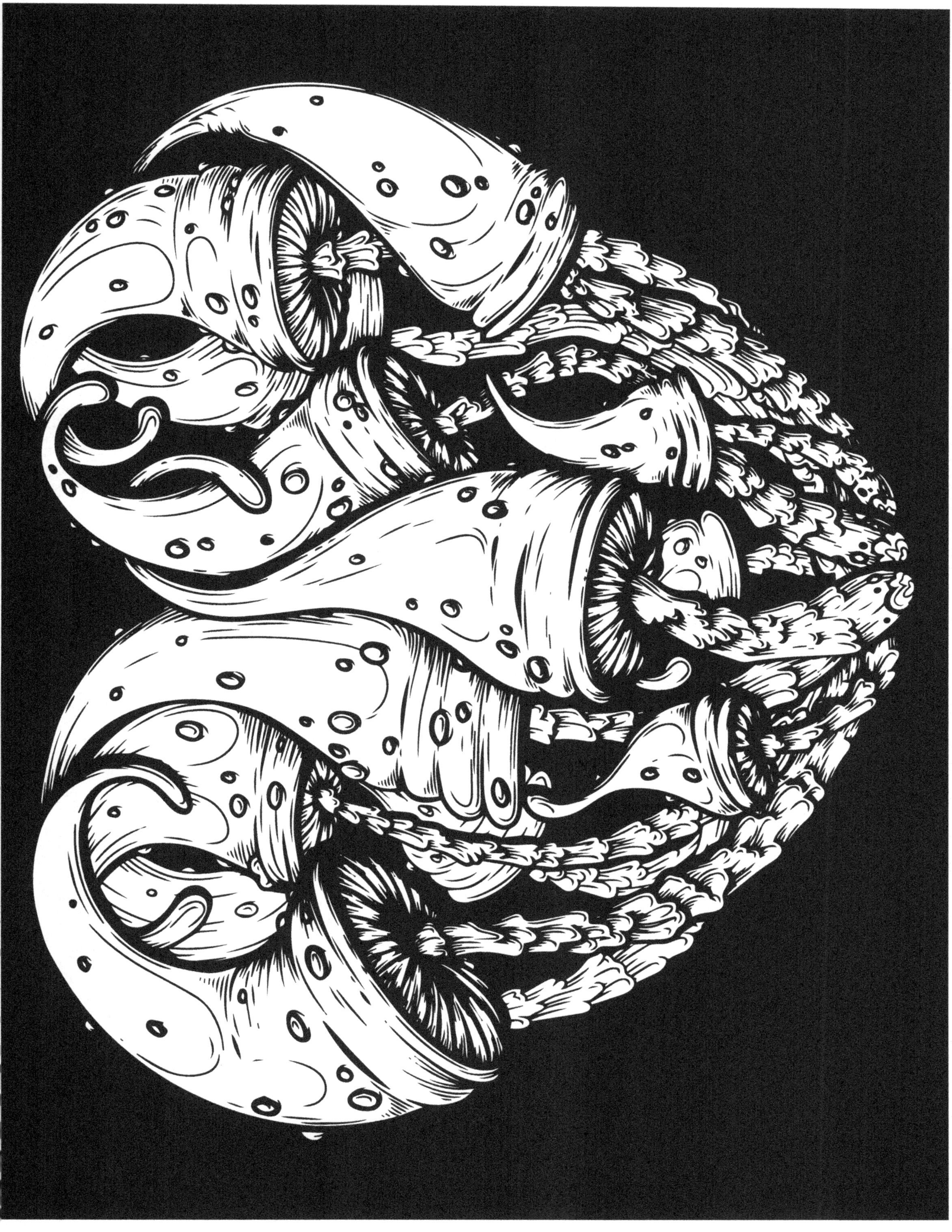

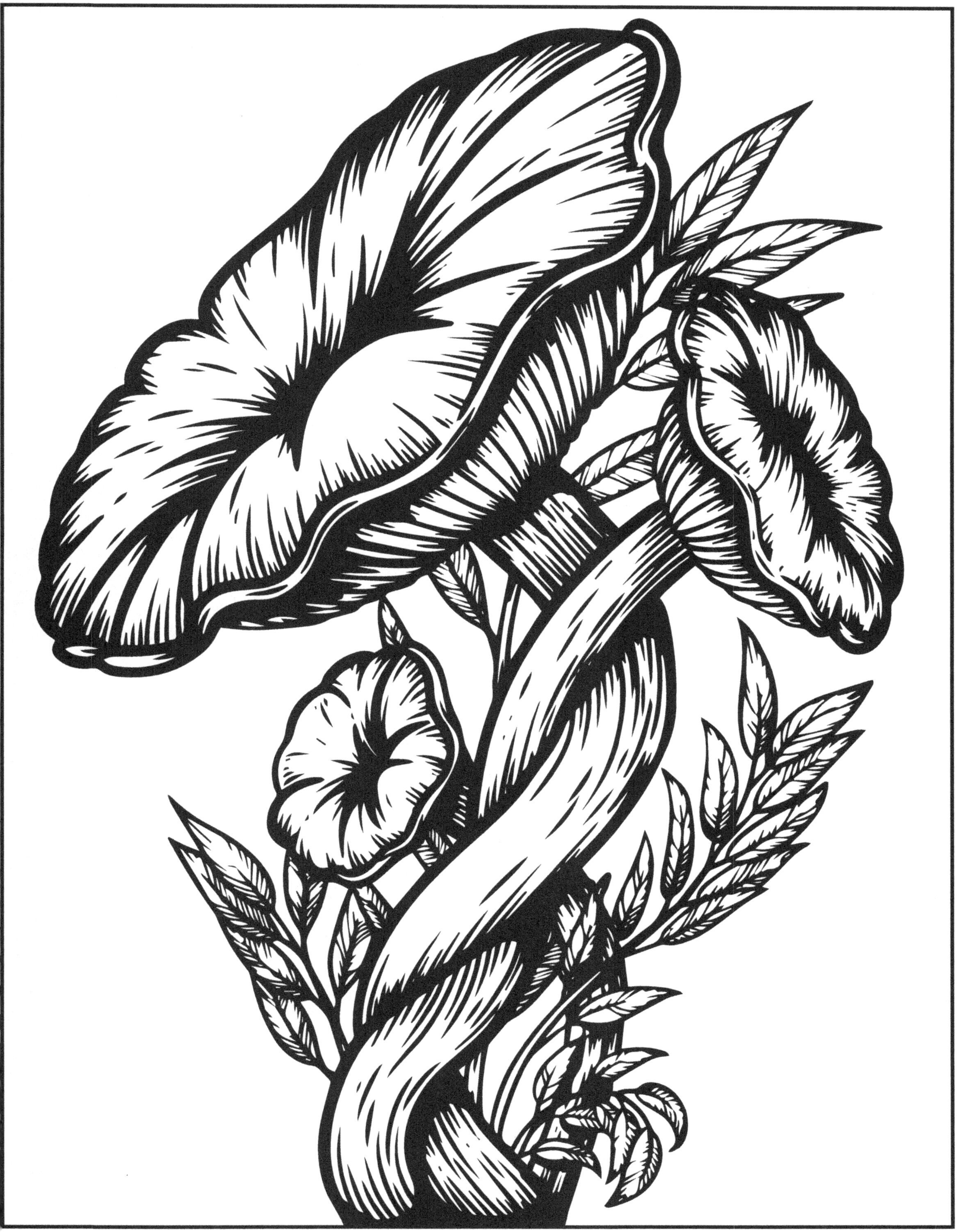

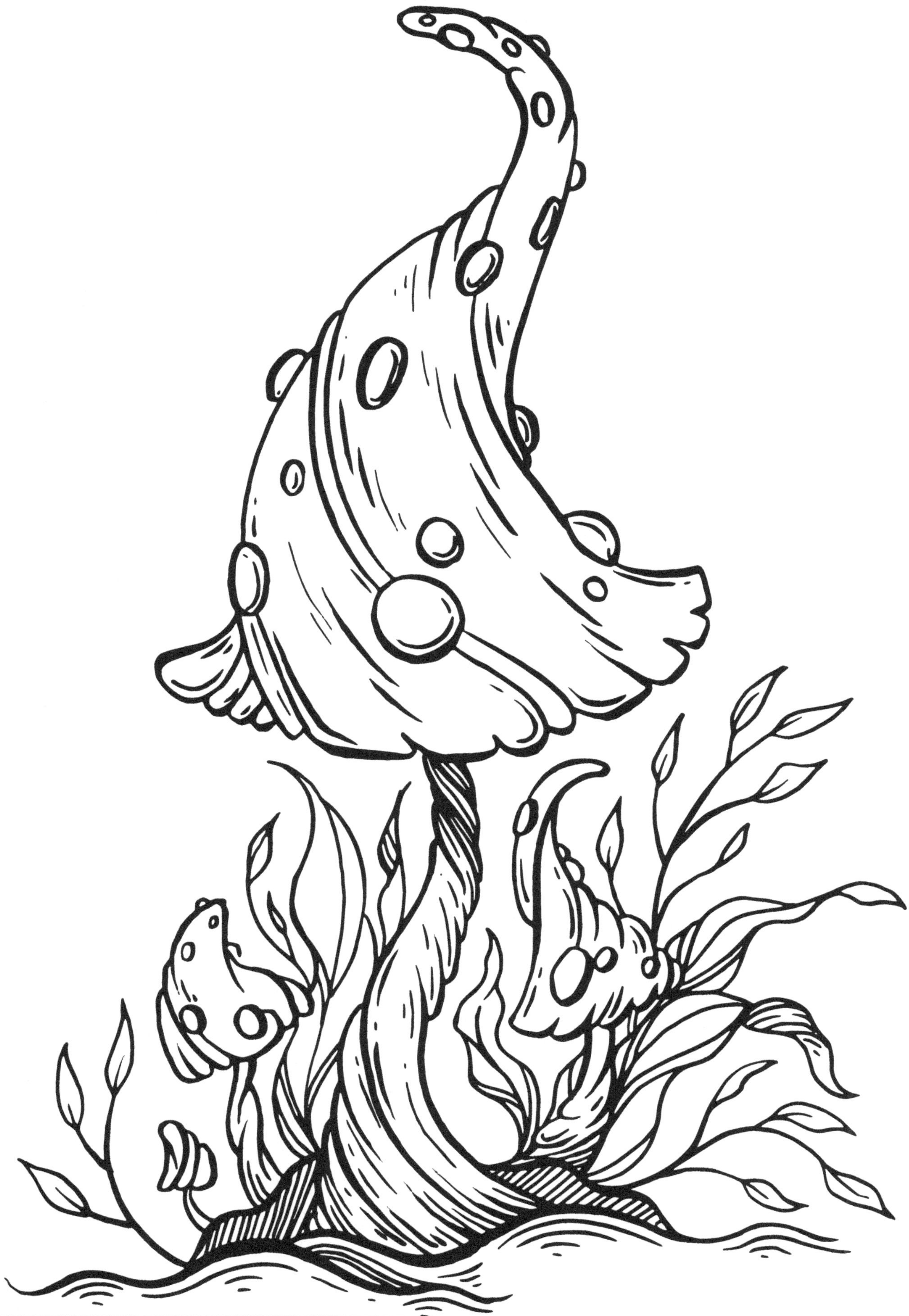

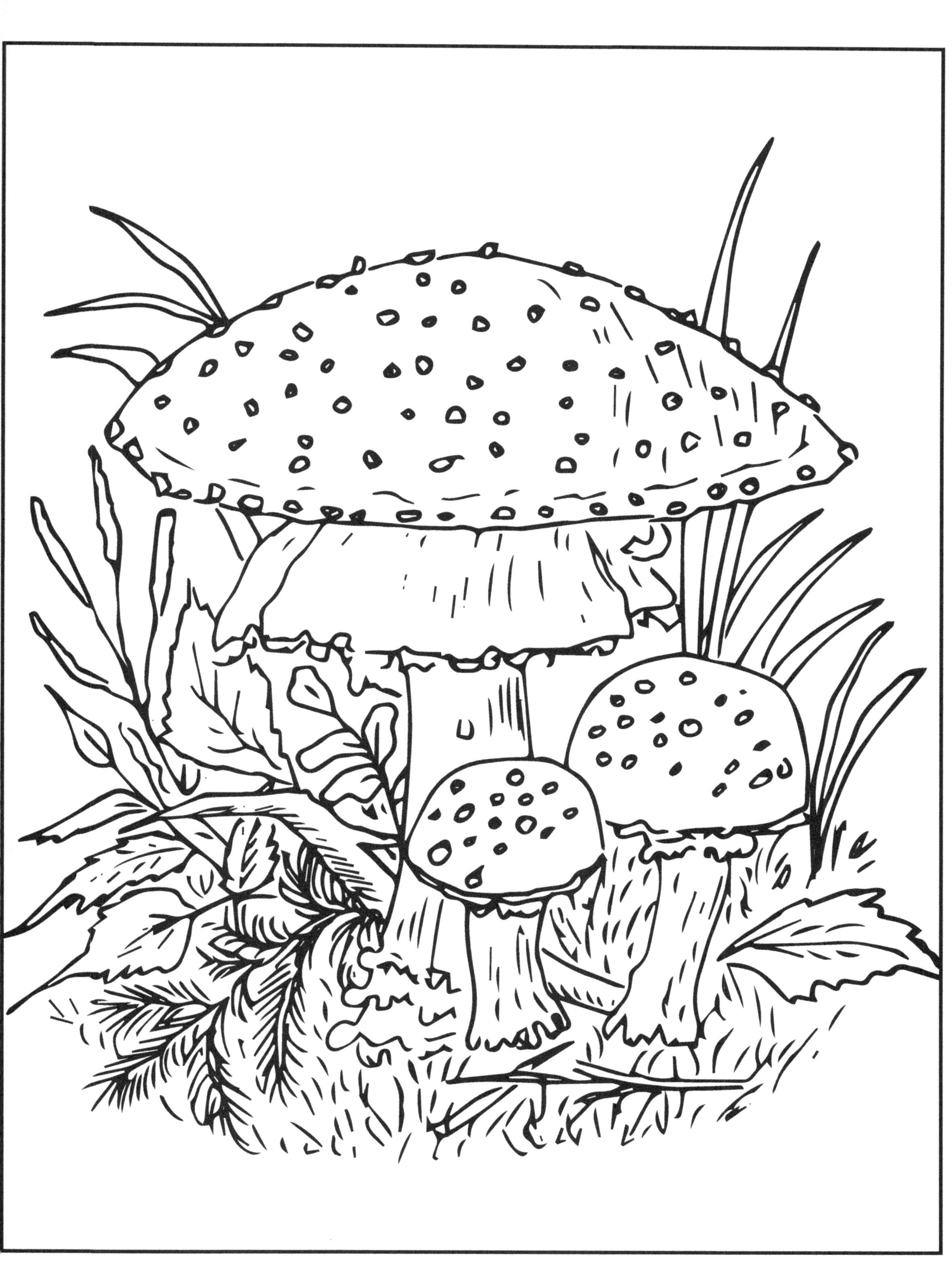

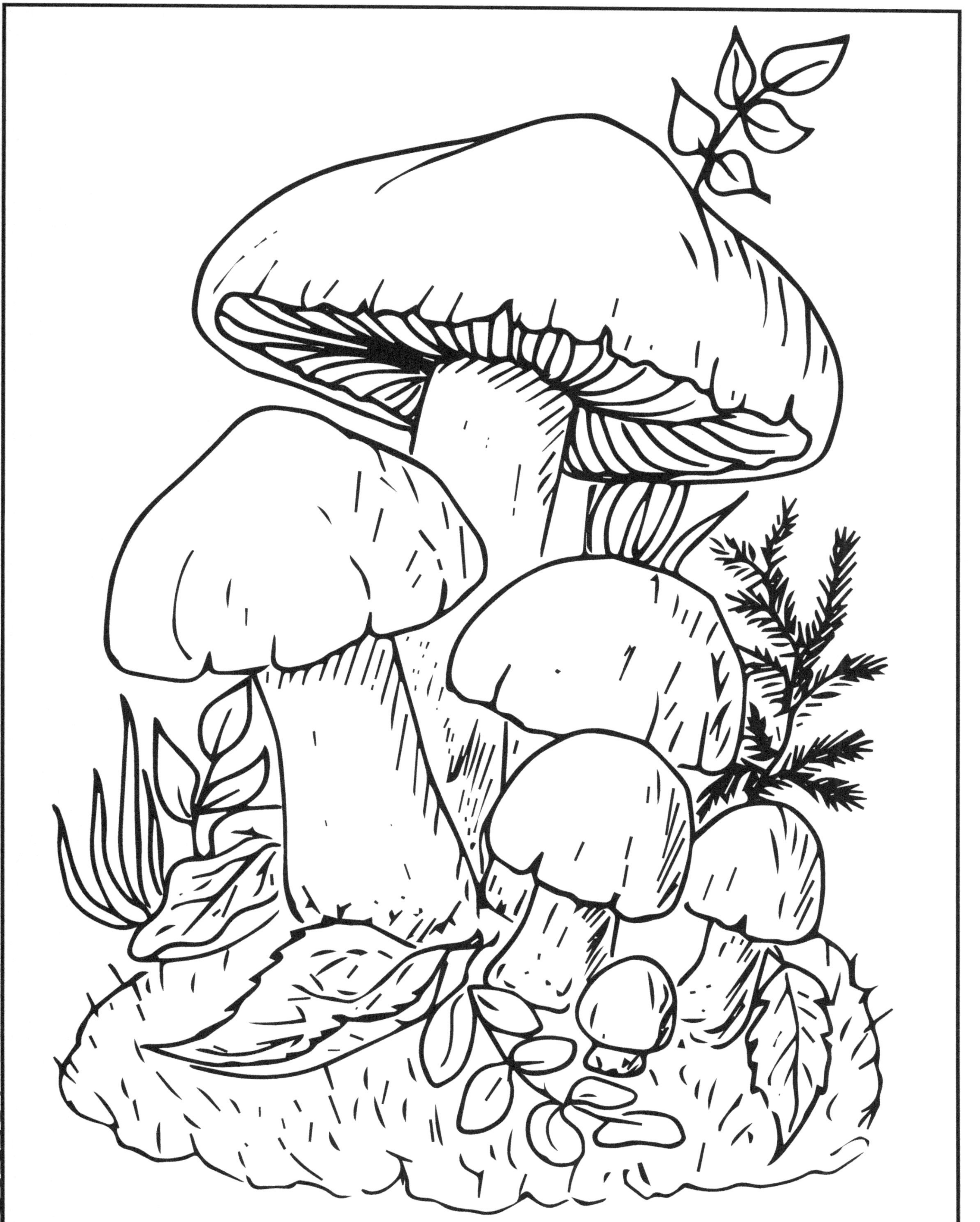

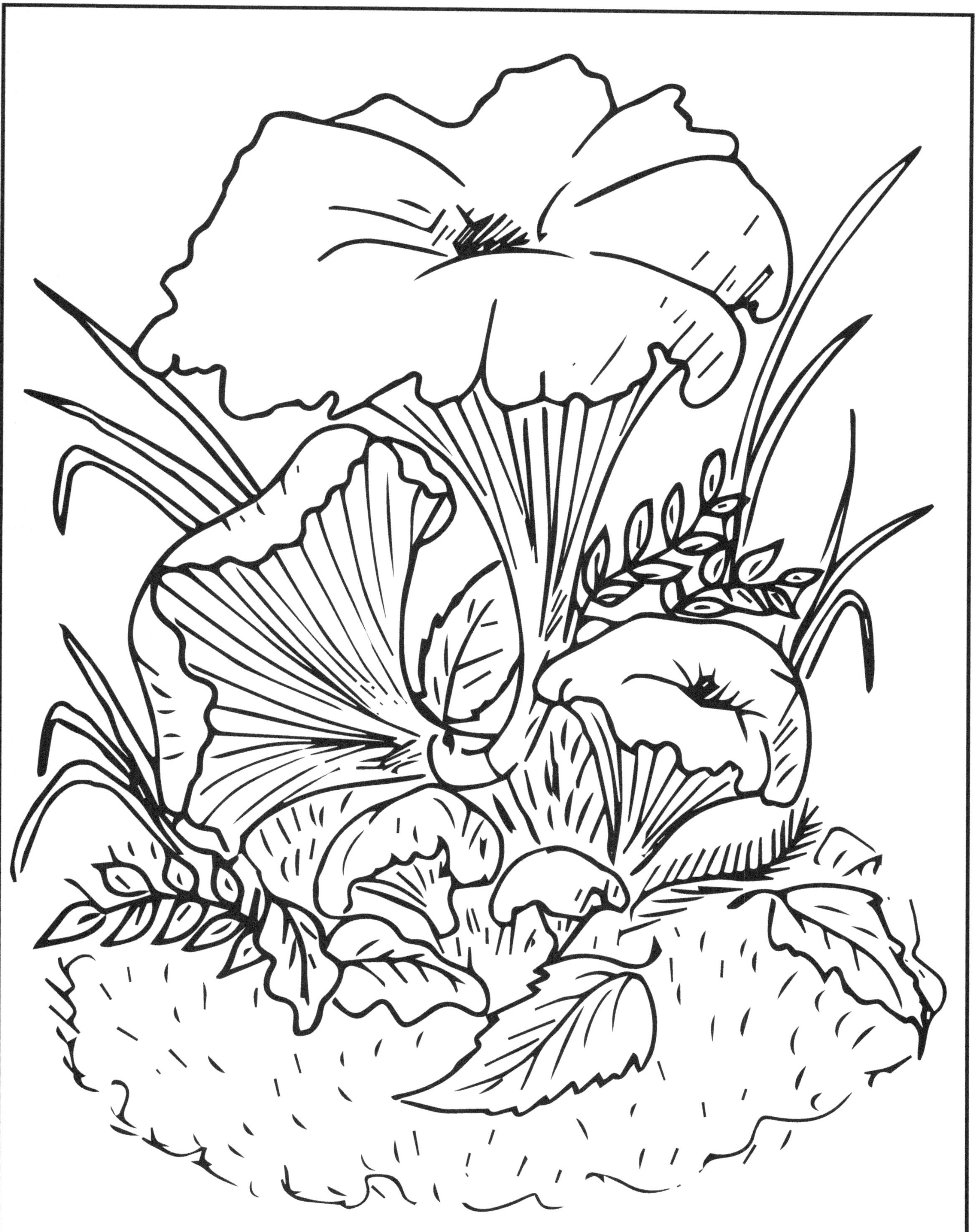

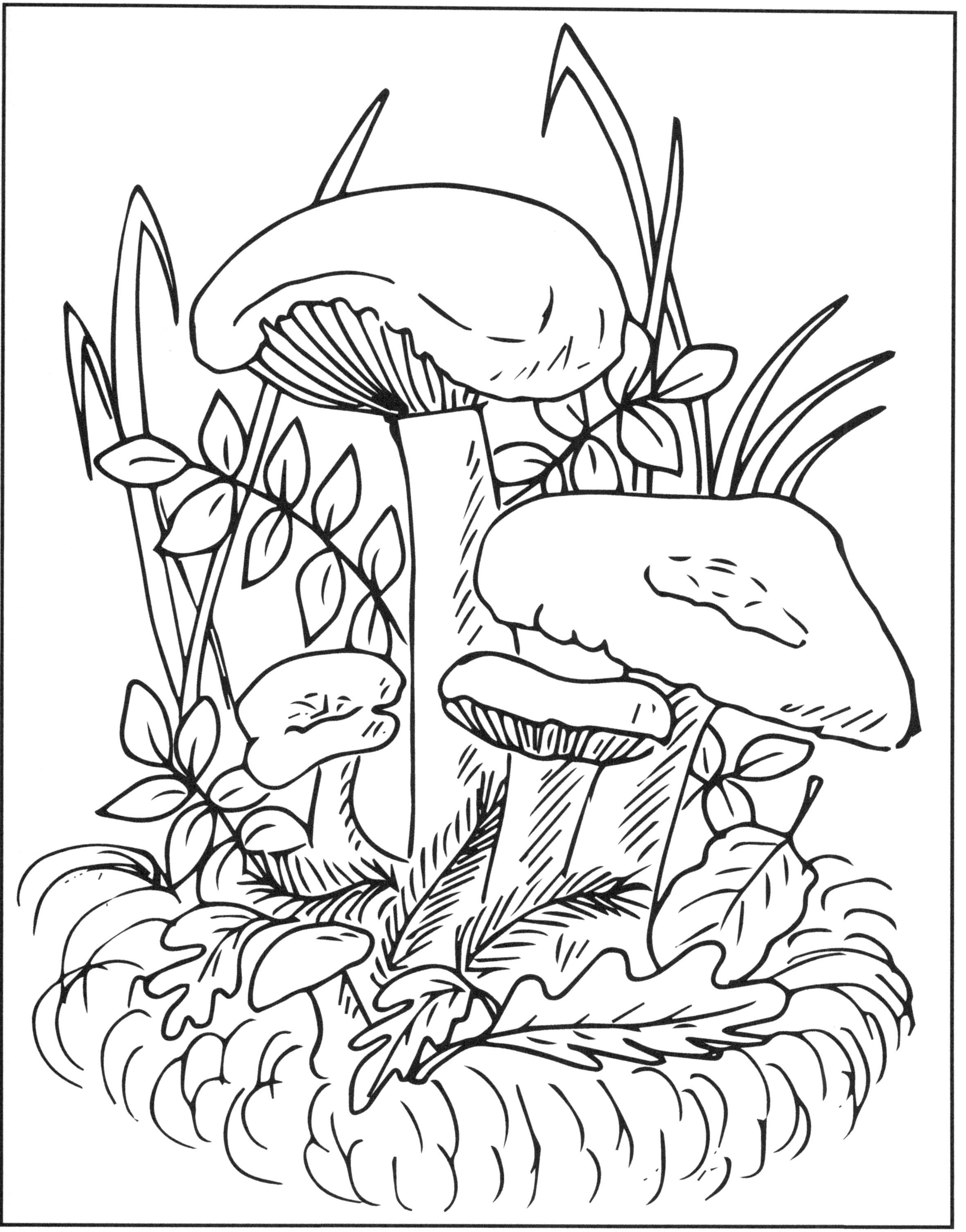

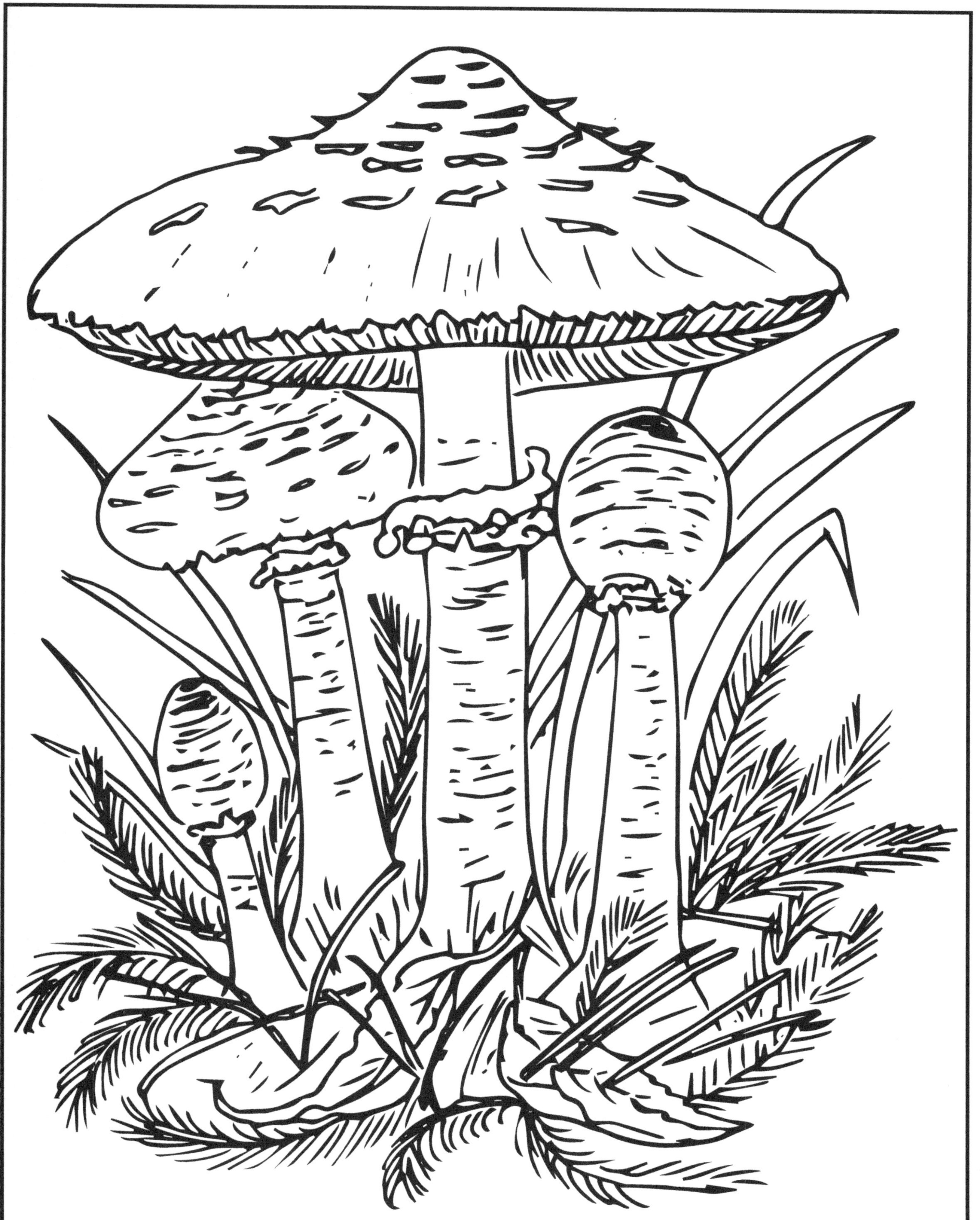

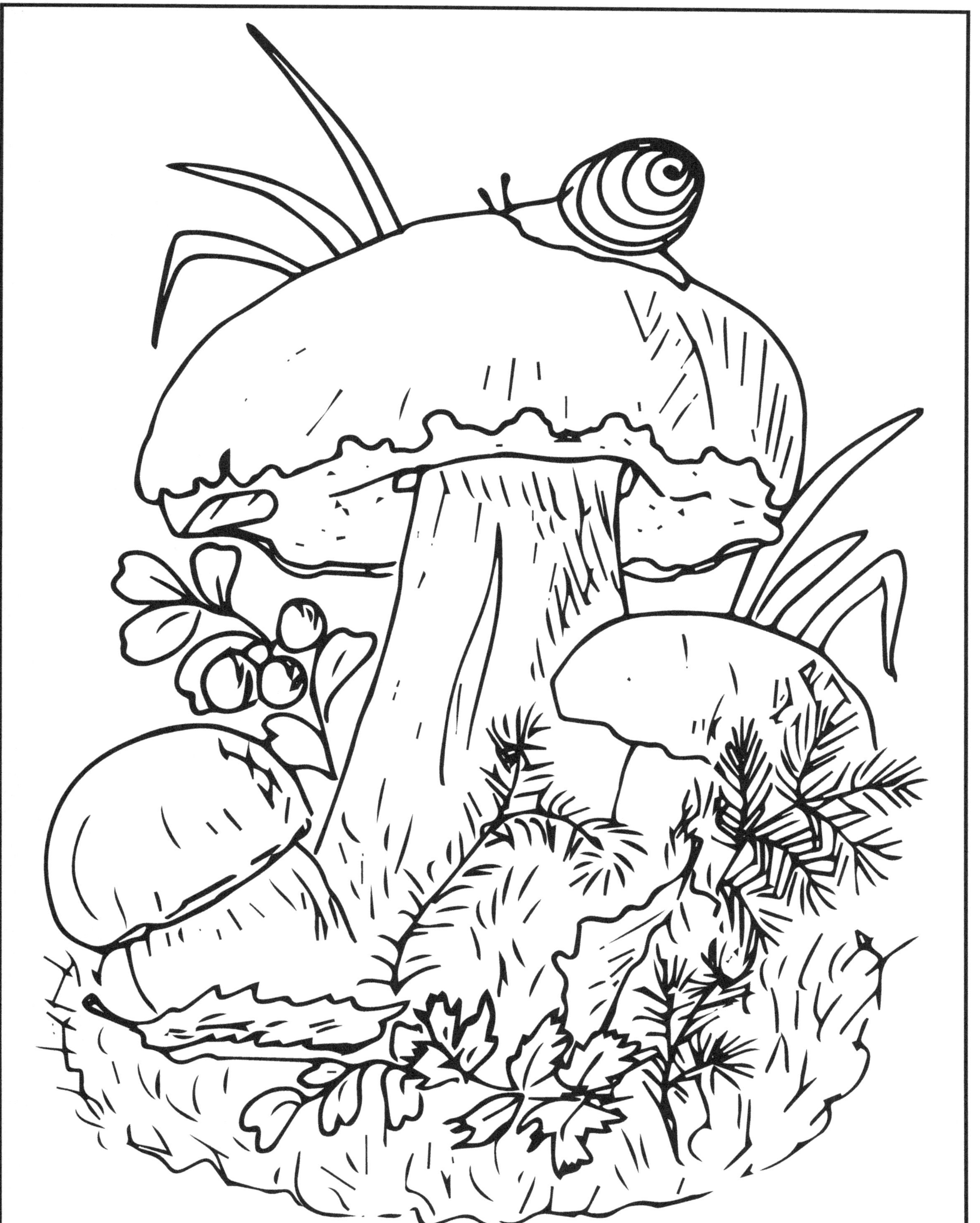

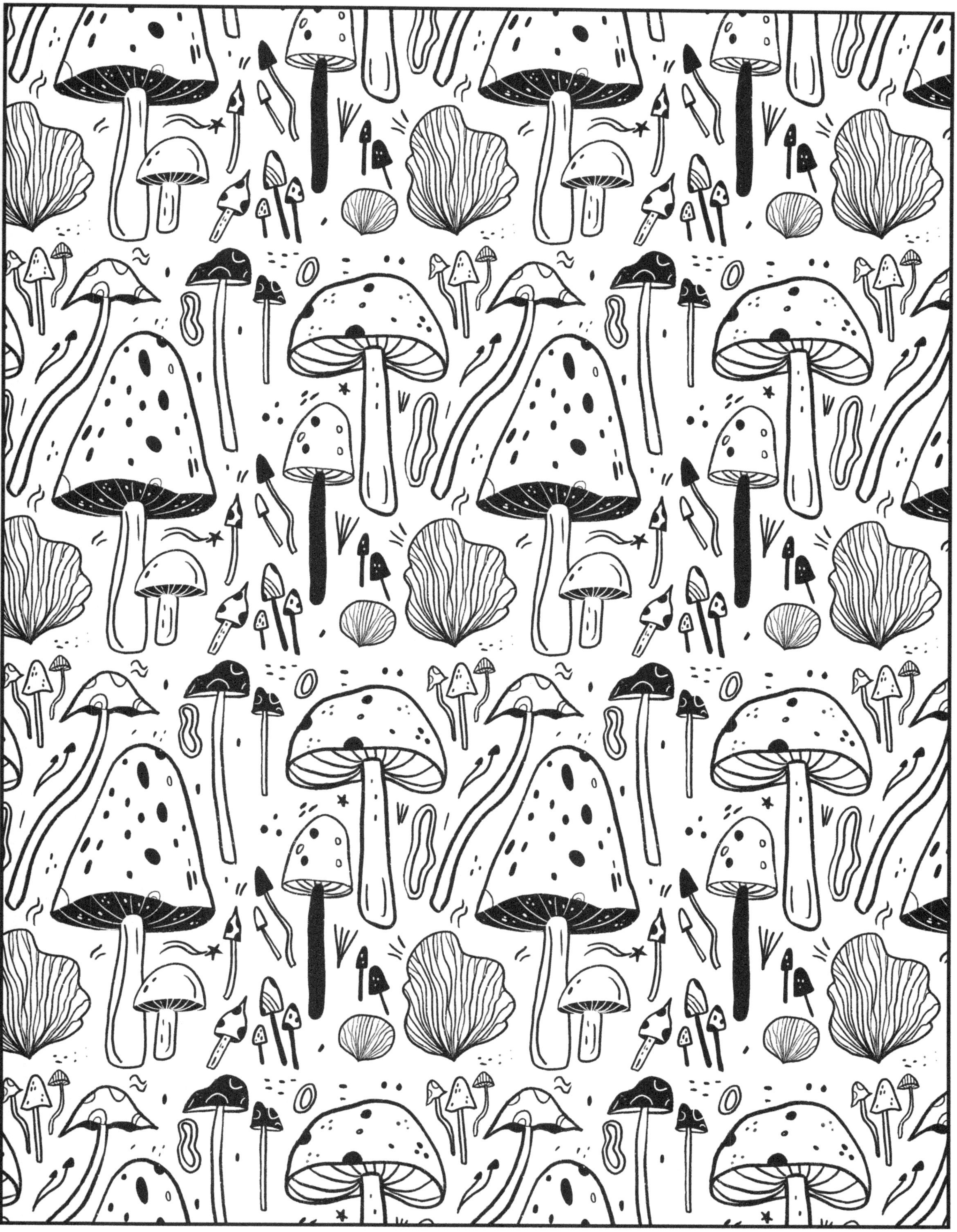

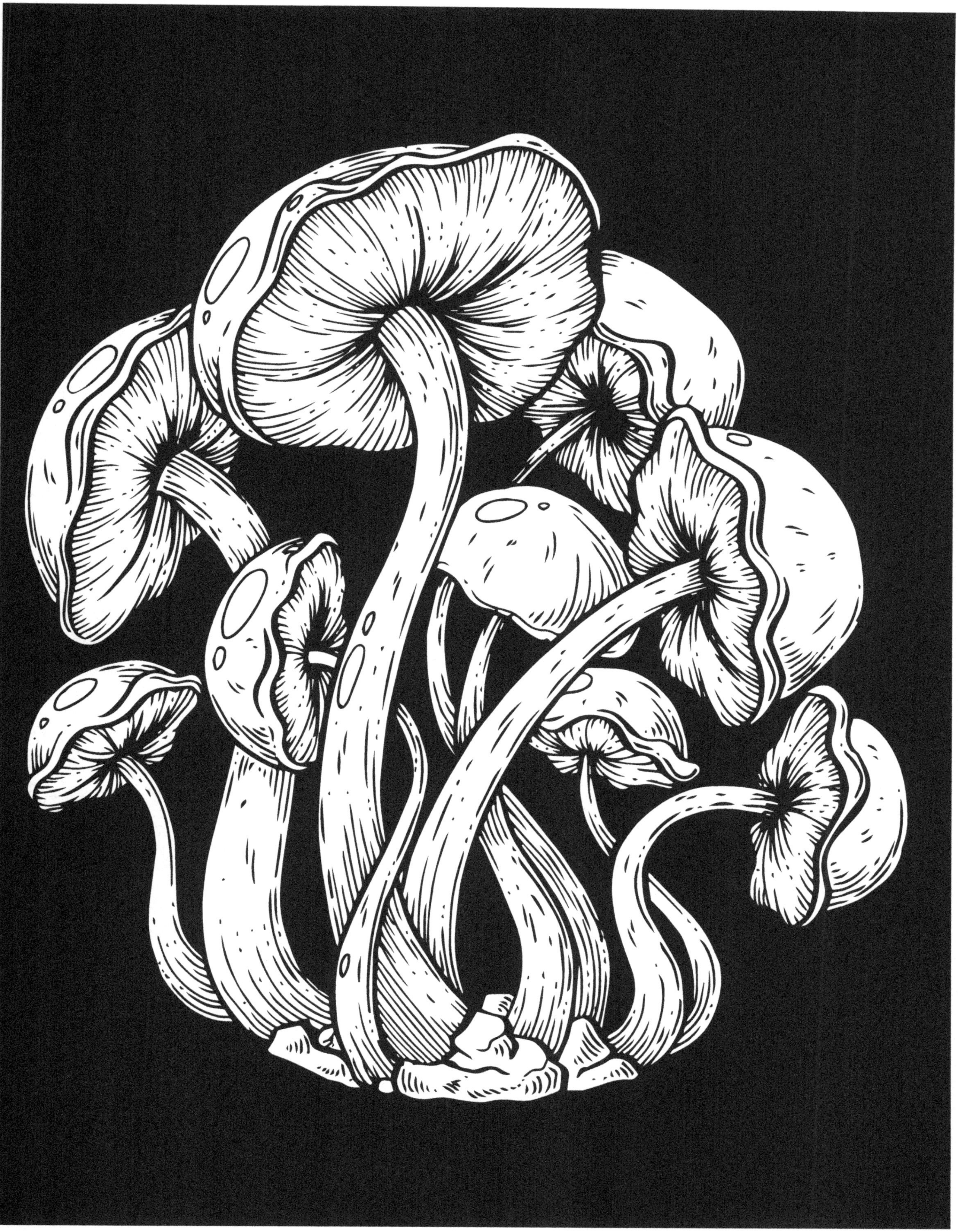

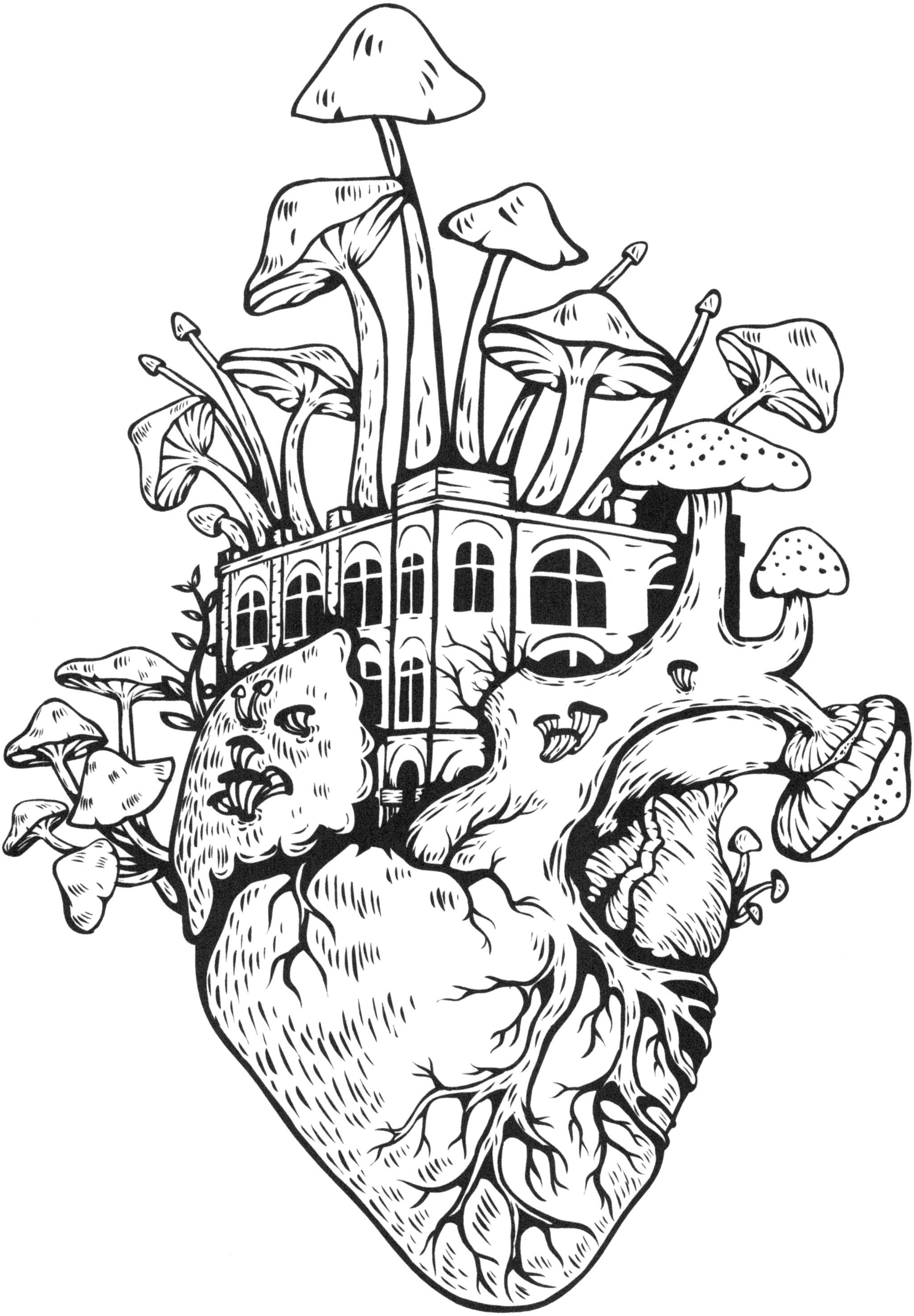

Made in the USA
Las Vegas, NV
16 November 2025

34151028R00037